I HAVE MADE IT THROUGH THE RAINBOW

Susan Willetts

authorHOUSE®

AuthorHouse™ UK Ltd.
500 Avebury Boulevard
Central Milton Keynes, MK9 2BE
www.authorhouse.co.uk
Phone: 08001974150

First published by AuthorHouse   8/24/2010

ISBN: 978-1-4520-6576-2 (sc)

This book is printed on acid-free paper.

To my beautiful angel charlotte my patient and encouraging husband mick and in memory of my late mother Evelyn Morris who inspired me to start writing poetry.

Contents

I have made it through the rainbow

I have made it through the rainbow,
I have made it through the storm,
Although it was rough and windy,
At times I couldn't find my way,
The sun shone through,
As God he paved the way,
Though it seemed the clouds would never disappear,
A still quiet voice said trust and be still and if you have ears let them hear,
Then suddenly the door opened by his mercy and his grace,
The clouds of doubt were far removed as I caught a glimpse of that heavenly place,
Then instead of raindrops of tears there were rivers of joy,
As once again I thank him and trust him with my life,
I have learnt that its on him I must rely and not keep asking when the storms abounding,
Please God tell me why.

Hope

If I can hold hope in my hand,
If I can have enough faith to believe even if it is as small as a grain of sand,
If I can love and learn to live,
If I can let bygones be bygones and try to forgive,
If I can see solutions in problems and not the other way round,
If I can gain sanity and not hear a sound,
If I can strive for peace and find the rainbows gold,
If I can retain the good times and remember them when I am old,
If I can see the sunshine and banish the rain,
If I can climb mountains and block out the pain,
Then I can start to recover and can face a new day,
Then I can face tomorrow and continue on my way,
If someone walks with me and we help each other to smile,
Then I know that I am living and that life is worthwhile.

The voice of peace

I dreamt I heard the voice of peace, travelling with the wind,
As peace moved the winds of time they whispered of centuries past,
Past winds from north, south, east and west, while prayers like bellows
fuelled the winds of change, as angels moved clouds of doubt and the winds
passed through their wings,
I dreamt I heard the voice of peace travelling with the waves, like the oceans
tides of change washed and cleansed pebbles of the past, as peace glistened
like golden beaches,
Angels watched as time ebbed and flowed,
I dreamt I saw the hand of peace as it touched every heart and mind,
Men laid aside their guns and swords as their souls no longer sighed,
As men laid aside their differences angels wept tears of joy,
I dreamt I saw the hand of peace extended to the nations, while men
grasped hope as angels sang Gods praises,
I dreamt I'd seen the face of peace as vibrant as the sun,
While children's smiles of sun rays melted mankind's years of hatred,
I dreamt I'd seen the face of peace as children's laughter filled the air,
While angels could be seen smiling as they watched the innocence of
childhood,
As I awake my dreams remain and peace still strives to make heaven and
earth equal,
While angels wait and watch north, south, east and west,
As the voice of peace hopes mankind ends his plight and lays the past to
rest.

Love

Love is like a rose beautiful and fragrant,
It's scent permeating everywhere,
Transforming peoples lives from buds into full blooming flowers,
Love is like a sunrise bringing light and brightness,
Where otherwise here would be darkness,
Love is in the touch of a hand, in a gentle word in a smile,
Love is like the new life of spring bringing birth, growth, creation,
Love is like summer it has warmth, radiance, its rays bring the world into
full bloom,
Love's voice can be heard can be heard in the dawn chorus like the birds it
declares its presence,
It can be heard in the gentle breeze through the trees on an autumn's day,
Its power gently stirs all who see its movement,
Love is the very essence of life, without love life loses its living and becomes
existing,
Where I ask does love start, where does it end? The answer is infinite,
Who is the composer of life's symphony? I do not find the answer from
mankind, or from my life on earth,
I find myself looking to the heavens, in this entire expanse of sky and stars I
continue my souls search,
I hunger and thirst as I find more and more I'm pointed to a master creator,
How else could love continue no matter where I look to the heavens or
earth? Love continues its composition,
I find God is Love, the Alpha and the Omega.

Do not be afraid

Do not be afraid for I am right by your side,
Do not be bound by turmoil or tears that you have cried,
Although you fear I have left you,
When you struggle from within,
You now have the opportunity daily to walk without being a slave to sin,
I have called you for a purpose,
To live a life of quiet repose,
To wait upon the Lord until the time has come,
To renew your strength and soar on eagles wings,
For it is in the valley that my restoration begins,
My healing is then completed and victory in me is won,
For I am your lord Jesus, your saviour and Gods one and only son.

I praise God

I praise god with all of my heart and from the depths of my soul,
Never before have I known such love as he has shown,
Before I met God I was all on my own,
Leaping from crisis to crisis life just didn't make sense,
With the world on my shoulders problems seemed so immense,
I did not know where to turn or where to go,
How I coped without him I just don't know,
I had endless days of uncertainty and nights of despair,
My life seemed in ruins and I did not really care,
How could anyone love me with the things I had said and done,
It was then God showed the love of the son,
The battle that had been raging inside me had already been won,
I was to come to him with my problems, my worries, my woes,
He said he would defeat them and all my foes,
Now the past cannot bind me and the futures a friend,
The Lords right beside me and to this there's no end,
He provides comfort and forgiveness for all of my sins,
Satan is defeated no battle he ever wins.

Hope

When I have no hope,
You are my hope,
When I have no courage,
You are my courage,
When I lose my strength,
You are my strength,
When there is no way you are the way,
When I feel lost you guide my steps and direct me,
When I am at my lowest ebb,
That's when you are closer than I could ever truly comprehend.

If you are feeling lonely

If you are feeling lonely and rejected then bring it to the Lord,
Arm yourself with Gods mighty sword,
Bring your worries to him they will never be ignored,
Rest in Gods peace and love and hold him by the hand,
There is no problem big or small that he does not understand,
Remember as you walk along life's path you are never on your own,
For the Lord is right beside you in places that are unknown,
He will never desert you or turn you away,
Just believe in his promises each and every day,
Then joy will flow like honey and in his presence you will stay,
You can not change the past and it should have no hold,
Step forth with Jesus show him you are bold,
Look daily to Jesus you can not go wrong,
With the holy spirit he will help you grow strong,
He will give you faith to move mountains and help you to cross rivers so deep,
Please do not despair you are one of his sheep and safe in his keep,
So sleep well tonight and know you are loved and wake in the morn,
Ready to serve him and to face the new dawn.

Through the rain

Through the rain I can see the sunshine,
Through the tears I can feel the joy,
Though my heart cannot comprehend the heartache,
I know in the presence of God I am truly loved,
Though I am weak and broken hearted,
Though I feel I have failed,
God I know is forever beside me and its for his
Righteousness, his kingdom, his glory,
That his will in time will prevail,
For the battle set before us,
Has in heaven already been won.
For God uses the hard times to refine to shape us,
To bring us closer to his son.

Although it is hard

Although it is hard Lord this battle I will win,
For when you died on the cross Lord you overcame sin,
You gave me your life so I could have mine,
No love that could equal yours so divine,
You overcame death you paid the price,
You gave up this worldly kingdom made the sacrifice,
Now your heavenly kingdom is justly restored,
Where you are worshipped by angels and rightly adored.

Thank you for the day

Thank you for the day you have given me,
Thank you for the blessings,
Definitely given overflowing from thee,
Thank you for the sunshine filled days,
With your nature speaking clearly of your loving ways,
Thank you for creation for me to enjoy,
Thank you for all you have given in this world,
For my senses to employ,
As I see in nature all the wondrous miraculous things,
My heart bursts with joy and I am pointed to heavenly thoughts as my heart sings,
I remember the times when I did not know thee,
I walked the earth spiritually blind,
For I did not what it meant to be totally free,
Now I know you I am free indeed,
To know you are the planter of creation and of every seed,
You are the creator of all animals and every ones designed by you,
Every single flower you have made and every single rainbow and with it
colours in every single hue,
One day I will see your glory in its entirety,
In heaven, creation on earth will seem like scarcity,
Help me to appreciate your beauty of all you have caused to be,
To taste in all its goodness for all eternity.

I am close

I am close to you I am closer than you think,
All of you that are thirsty come to the well and drink,
Al of you that are truly hungry come to me for heavenly bread,
All of you who are lost on the path that you tread,
Come to me and receive rest,
All of you that are lonely whilst travelling from east, south,
North and west,
Come to me for I am closer than you think,
All of you in trials and with burdens come to me,
Lighten your load,
I am your Lord, your saviour,
You are not on your own I am right next to you,
For I am closer than you think,
There is not a prayer I cannot answer,
I am your Lord, I am your comforter, I am your counsellor,
You matter to me,
I am closer than you think,
I am near to you,
I am not distant,
I am closer than you think,
Open your eyes, your ears, your heart,
I am closer than you think,
Please rest a while, I am Jesus I am closer than you think,
Those of you who are truly thirsty come to the well and drink,
For I am closer in today, in your life,
I am closer than you think.

If I could dream

If I could dream of a life beyond the walls of doubt and the walls of fear,
Where God is close and forever near,
Where love abounds and gives me cheer,
If I could make the step beyond trusting only myself,
Entrust to him all aspects of my health,
Give him all I hold so dear,
If I could see an idyllic plain where the tastes and sights of heaven remove
the pangs of pain,
If I could know once again Love, hope and peace,
I would soon be well and finally have a release
If I could grasp the wondrousness of God and touch the hand of Jesus,
Then Gods healing could be ministered to me,
Then I could live be alive once more and in his arms be light or spirit and
once again be free.

Fountain of life

Fountain of life living in me,
Replenishes my thirst for life,
Give me the desire to break forth and free,
Remember no more child the life that you lived,
Its forgiven, forgotten now you belong to me,
The good Lord says although you struggled and fought through difficult times and tried different ways,
When I revealed myself to you that's when your life began to change,
Living water overflowing the start of something new,
I wanted to take the pain away and give you a life afresh and to renew,
I could see your every move as you walked along the path,
But forgiveness flowed from within my heart and love for you I felt instead of wrath,
Now in my kingdom you have transferred from dark to light,
Keep on persevering and drinking from the well and this will be my hearts delight.

you are not gone

You are not gone, You are in one of heavens rooms,
Housed in a heavenly palace, Free from pain and anguish,
No longer groaning with life's burdens or cares,
You are now holding Jesus hand, Smiling and laughing like you used to,
Young once again with a face like an angel,
This gives me comfort as I remember you as you was,
Vibrant full of life and vigour without tears,
This is not the end for you have eternal life as Jesus promised,
I will see you one day perfect without blemish,
You will live on in my memories,
You will always be in my thoughts and prayers,
You have renewed your strength like the eagle,
And one day I will soar with you in our creators heaven,
When I see blue skies I will always remember you,
As I am reminded of you loving the sunshine,
Soaking up nature, I will see you again for you will live on through me,
I will never forget that you gave me the gift of life,
You are not gone, You are sleeping,
One day I will be able to hold you in my arms and tell you once again that I
love you.

Oasis

Sun drenched land parched and arid,
As I trek for miles and miles,
Although this toil I have greatly parried,
I will keep walking until god breaks through, As the sun shines down from heaven,
As I almost lose my way,
I thank God for the bread of heaven,
It uplifts my soul and sustains me for the day,
As the palm trees appear far away,
As I long to quench my thirst,
Rivers from God overwhelm me,
As arid deserts of life spring forth and burst forth water,
It creates new life ever flowing,
My heart isn't bursting forth with sadness and sorrow,
But its filled with joy for now and tomorrow,
It isn't aching as it did, but my heart is ever knowing,
I can face the future and I can come away from the rocks from whence I hid.

In my quietest moments

In my quietest moments,
Often at my deepest need,
When my heart is at its most silent,
The Lord he plants his seed.
The seed of encouragement not to my faith,
As on the cross I see him bleed,
As I see him up there suffering,
How can I doubt his love for me?
Would a mere man die?
So he could set the whole world free?
When my heart is aching and all my
Tears have been cried,
I find my savior wipes my tears away,
And suddenly my eyes have dried.
The barriers of blind heart and mind,
Now are seen as far behind.
For I truly want to do god's will,
When Jesus makes my heart become still,
Then true joy I start to find.

Although

Although I cannot comprehend how I am feeling today,
I know you are my Lord and that you are the way,
I know that if I trust you with my innermost fears,
You can wipe the tears away and stress built up over the years,
You can heal what is broken,
You can make me whole,
For when we find we are struggling,
You sustain our very soul.

Make me whole

Make me whole Lord,
Make me whole,
Renew my heart Lord,
Restore my soul,
Renew my mind Lord,
Renew my mind,
Help me leave my troubles behind,
Give me peace Lord,
Give me peace,
Clothe me in your shepherds fleece,
Give me love Lord,
Give me love,
Sanctify me from God above,
Stay with me Lord,
Stay with me
I pray your spirit with me will forever be,
Give me joy Lord,
Give me joy,
I know your friendship will never lie,
I thank you Lord for loving me,
Till we meet in heaven for eternity.

The River of life

I was walking along the journey of life,
Wondering what it all meant in the scheme of things,
Thinking why was I here and did life just happen when suddenly I came to
a river,
It was deep cool and clear the sunlight was reflecting on the water,
Making it glisten and sparkle like a jewel,
I gazed at the beautiful scene for a while and reflected on my journey so far,
I realized that I had been thirsting all my life,
I realized that nothing had quenched my thirst,
I had been searching for something to fill my soul,
Deep within I realized my soul was crying out for living water,
I knelt down by the waters edge and drank as though I had never drank before,
I found that it was not just a physical need that was being met but a deep
longing was being filled,
There was a desire to know God and Jesus was being stirred up within me,
Jesus said to the woman at the well that he would give living water,
Now at the river I had found living water that overflows the cup of joy,
I now no longer wonder what life is all about as I have found the water giver
and the river of life lies within me.

I wonder

I wonder what God looks like when he smiles does his face shine radiantly
and as brightly as the sun?
I wonder what God looks like when he weeps tears of joy do the tears fall to
the ground like a waterfall?
I wonder what Gods face is like when he sees me on the earth below, does
he rejoice with the angels and have a song stored in his heart?
I wonder what his embrace is like as his heavenly arms touch me with an all
encompassing love,
I am convinced when I look at the painstaking way he has placed stars in
the universe,
When he blesses the earth with sun and rain that his arms surely convey love,
What does Gods voice sound like when he whispers do the trees gently sway
with the breeze?
I wonder am I like the mountain broken yearning to be in the potters hands?
One day I will see God and meet him face to face with no more wondering,
I will know beyond my wildest dreams beyond a shadow of a doubt that
God is love,
As sure as night follows day,
As sure as the oceans are governed by the moon,
I will know in all fullness that God is the alpha and omega and that he
expresses love that has no end.

Life beyond measure

I have life beyond measure,
It is you Lord that I treasure,
You mean the world to me,
For all the riches are mine eternally,
In a heavenly kingdom for you haven chosen me,
By your grace and mercy it was meant to be,
I love you Lord teach me to love you more,
Teach me to ask seek knock on you my saviours door,
I will run the race without fear for there is nothing I cannot face with you holding my hand,
There is no problem you do not understand,
As you sit upon your heavenly throne,
I can face much more with you than I could ever do on my own,
I am truly rich I am an heir of your love,
I am an heir of your peace like a dove,
Yes I am richer than any earthly king,
I join in adoration of you as heavenly angels as t heir hearts bursting with joy do sing.

The Garden of peace

I was walking through a garden,
Holding your hand and you holding mine,
We were talking about our precious memories together,
we talked about the dreams we held so dear to our hearts,
As we walked through the garden smelling the beautiful roses in full bloom,
As we were looking at the butterflies and the birds,
As we rested in the garden a while and felt the gentle breeze
As we remembered our love for each other when we first met
And remember now that first love we had for each other remains strong
We can face together what tomorrow may bring
With love and peace in our hearts
That garden where we first met can be ours once again.

I am truly rich Lord

I am truly rich Lord I could not ask for more,
One day I will see you as I walk through heavens door,
I will be with you forever for there will be no stormy weather,
Yes I am truly richer than before because in this life I have found you and
that's what I have been looking for,
Now I have found you Lord my life is complete and whole,
Teach me o Lord to love you with my mind my heart my soul,
I am rich beyond measure Lord I have more than gold,
For you are real to me and close to me,
You are not just a story that for centuries has been told,
I thank you for my days on earth as they unfold,
I know I can approach you and be bold,
So until we meet I will build riches that last eternally,
Thank you for making me free,
For I am not chained by sin anymore as daily I can walk with thee.

You are there

You are there when I wake up in the morning,
You are waiting for me to acknowledge your glorious presence,
You are waiting for me to converse with you,
You are waiting for me to give you thanks for the beautiful sunshine or the refreshing rain,
You are waiting for me to be given your many blessings,
To see you in the strangers smile,
To see your love demonstrated throughout all the earth,
To see new beginnings and to have the hope of a good day,
To see me following your ways,
You are there as the day closes in as dusk closes the sky's curtain,
I can have assurance and certainty that your hand protects,
I know that you are always there in the sunshine in the rain in the tempest,
You never leave us you are always there,
You are always ready to walk with us along life's journey,
You are there in all things good and all things challenging,
My prayer now is that I am here to seek your will.

Rain

Lord you are here with me in all of this rain,
Although I cannot see you through the torrents I can feel your presence
taking away the pain,
I can see that you are guiding me, directing me and showing me the way,
You are covering me with heavenly arms both in the night and day,
I only have to reach out to you,
I only have to call your name,
I know you will help me in the tempest,
For you remain the same,
For you are always true,
Even though I am scared and I cry out to you,
I know the storms and rains will not last forever,
I know I will make it through,
For the storms are refining and shaping me,
They are making me grow and I am feeling closer to you,
I am changing in my deepest part I am changing and becoming new,
I say rain fall down, rain fall down on me,
For when I am drenched in your presence I am totally free,
Its not that I like storms but with you holding me near,
The perfect love you show casts out all fear,
So when the rain comes down and come it will,
With you by my side I can know peace in my heart and be still,
Trusting in you Lord with my heart, my soul, my mind,
Walking through the storm Lord as I leave the last storm behind,
Knowing that the next storm I face Lord will not overwhelm,
For Lord I can rest assured that you will be at the helm,
Nothing will defeat me in the present or the past,
For you provide the shelter of an inheritance that will always last.

One moment

I want to live every moment to the full,
I want to grasp every second live it for God,
I want to give my all to his purpose and follow his plan,
I want to place my life in his hands and when doubt starts to surface replace it with a vision of I can,
To let people know that Jesus was not just a man,
I want people to know that Jesus was not just a man,
I want people to know he is in my heart changing ugliness to beauty and will not depart,
The yearning in my soul I do not want to stop,
I want to be on fire for my king,
I want my life to be overflowing as endless songs I sing,
I want to tell of Gods love for me,
Replacing bitterness for love so that all can see,
The wondrousness of God causing me to bloom like a beautiful flower to fulfil my destiny,
To declare nothing is impossible if we are in Gods precious hand,
Nothing will defeat us because he will always understand,
I want to be filled with passion and reach towards the skies,
I want to end the enemy's grasp and release his hold on lies,
Let god reign within my being,
Let him give me peace,
I want to hold his hand as I walk I want to be one of his sheep and do not want to weep,
I want to walk in victory and see his power release,
Until I am called back to heaven I am going to stand on the mountain top and declare all he has done for me,
I Know that he is close in even in my darkest days and that he has set me free,
At last my chains are broke and I am truly what God wants me to be.

Now I have you

Now I have you in my life Lord I Can live another day and not just exist,
I can have the opportunity to view this world through your eyes,
I can take in all its beauty and splendour and enjoy your blessings as it was intended,
I can have the opportunity to walk with you from the moment I awake,
Until the moment I fall asleep,
I can have the opportunity to be in your presence from the dawn of a new day to the setting of the sun and beyond,
I can have the opportunity to see the world through your perspective and not my own,
I can have the opportunity to rise above all that holds or attempts to hold me back,
By holding your hand mountains are but a hill disguised as an obstacle,
A hundred miles can seem but ten,
When my will reflects your will a thousand steps are but one,
As I reach my destination and know in my heart that the journey we have travelled on is called recovery,
I can have the opportunity to grasp life in all its essence once again,
I am not alone as before, this time I have a beautiful and wonderful companion.

I will cherish

I will cherish all that you have given me,
I will cherish all that I have been given by thee,
This means I am blessed indeed,
May my life be as seed that grows and a life
That gives you all the glory in full view,
I thank you that I can live again and it is all because of you,
As I am standing on the mountain top as my heart sings aloud with praise,
I thank you for the long sunshine filled and God blessed days,
As I build my life upon the ageless rock as you stand the test of time,
I thank you for choosing me that I am a guest at the banquet and you are
the finest wine,
I thank you that you are the bread of life,
I thank you I can spend with you eternity,
I thank you that I have crossed from dark to light and you have forgiven me,
I thank you for the day and night, the sun, the stars, the moon,
I thank you that one glorious day you will come back,
Let us hope and pray it will be soon,
Thank you for all the riches with you have chosen to light my soul,
Thank you for completeness in you Lord,
Thank you for making me whole,
I will cherish every moment, every single day you have given me,
I will walk by faith as now I am totally free.

As I was walking

As I was walking on earths dusty path,
I found a saviour who reaches out to me,
He bound my wounds and gently carried me in his arms,
The healing from Jesus that day was and is to come,
To all who believe Jesus is who he says he is and that he is
Gods only son and that one day he will return for us all to claim the victory
that has already been won.

My little angel

My little angel I am holding you in my arms,
I will cherish you for you are a gift from God,
As precious so wanted and I will encourage you in all that you want to
achieve and all that you want to be,
In all that God desires for you and all he wants to give,
I will be here for you to watch you grow and we can both learn along the way,
I will be here to build special memories and support you as you make your
way in the world,
I will be here no matter what life brings for I am your mom,
For God has truly blessed me and I will never forget this,
For you are a true treasure from heaven.

Oasis

Oasis of life that's what you are to me,
When I think the rivers run dry,
That's when I find you quench my thirst and replenish my soul by the palm tree,
As the sun beats down on my brow,
You send joyous honey with manna from heavens store,
As I search for you I find my hunger for you grows more and more,
Oasis of life springing from the well,
From desert experiences you never can tell,
Who we may meet that the Lord wants us to great,
To bring them to him and for them to listen at his feet,
If we cry out to Jesus he will hear our plea,
Restored overflowing,
brimming with happiness forgiven and free,
We can learn in the desert if we choose to try,
For it is in the dry season that god hears us and like eagles we start to fly,
He waters the ground when it is dry and pours out his love,
He surrounds his children with protection and gives peace like a dove,
If today you find yourself in the desert and God seems out of reach,
Remember it is in the desert that the Lord may want to teach,
To hold onto his promises to know that they are true,
For the inheritance to be claimed by me and you,
So we must never lose hope,
For in the dry and arid times God will help us to cope,
When we have rested and turned back to him,
We can turn back from the wilderness and true living can begin.

Beautiful day

I awoke early in the morning,
With a song deep within my heart,
Like a nightingale in full vocal array,
A joyous fountain of living water,
Welling inside my very soul burst forth,
At last I feel complete and whole,
Although my experiences have been difficult and arduous,
I now see a purpose for living,
I can see a reason for giving,
The past seems but a speck on the horizon soon to be forgot,
Even though the cost has been a lot,
As I see the Journey mapped before me which is prosperous not to gain
material wealth,
But to experience Gods love and spiritual health,
Thus every day I Commit my life to him,
I give him all my praise from deep within.
All that happened can be left at the cross,
All I can gain I Count as loss,
For to be in Gods presence is my hearts desire,
To be bathed with Gods holy fire,
To be spurred on to win the race,
To in my life seek Gods face.
So I can wake in the morning do his will,
Find peace of mind and for my heart to be still,
To do all in life he wants me to fulfil.

Under the shadow of your wings

I am under the shadow of your wings,
Where I am safe from harm,
When I am in your presence I feel your beautiful sense of calm,
When I am bathed in your love,
When I feel peace in my heart like that of a dove,
When I find shelter when you are so close,
Then I can find healing when I am in a state of quiet repose,
When I find your protection and nestle in your heavenly arms,
When I cease striving for trivial things and find that I can enter rest,
I can get to know my father know he loves me and that he alone knows
what is best.

Tired

I am feeling tired and weary,
My love of life has become a chore,
What once excited me lacks luster,
All in life has become such a bore,
I know I shouldn't feel this way Lord,
I know that I should be filled with the joys of spring,
I know my heart should be overflowing with praises heartfelt,
Giving thanks for the abundance of life that everyday can anew bring,
I am feeling irritable in my spirit,
I am feeling tired but cannot rest,
I am tired from the trial and the test,
I know Lord I need your guidance,
For to my spirit you will attest that I need to place my trust in you and those you entrust to make me well again,
To fully dwell in your resting place and shelter and my health regain.

I am waiting

I am waiting for the glorious day when my saviour will return to earth,
When angels will spread their wings as the trumpet calls,
When the Lords face will shine as brightly as the sun,
When the battle of good and evil will well and truly be won,
I am waiting for the day when Jesus will hold me in his arms and love and peace will fill my being,
A day of wondrousness happenings that never before has been seen,
I am waiting for the day that Jesus will call his sheep and tenderly say their name,
As for now I will boldly declare the Lord and the reason that he came,
To take the sin of the world of you and I,
He hung on a cross so we would not have to die,
For if we confess with our mouth he is Lord we have an eternity,
With which to spend to which there is no end,
Each day I pray that my faith will grow and grow,
So to other people I will be able to show the love Jesus has for them,
So that they will too come to know,
Let me be like Jesus let me be his hand his eyes his feet,
Let me walk in victory until that glorious day when the saviour and I meet.

This day I will live for you

This day I pledge I will live for you,
This day I will follow you in the ways you want me to,
This day I will place you first in every thing,
I will change the focus from anxiety,
To walking with joy in my heart everlasting and my soul will sing,
This is not because of what I have done for you,
But because of what you have done for me,
For when I set aside my worldly fears,
You bring your healing for all those years,
That I followed you with a heavy heart,
This day if I choose to put you first,
It can be the beginning of a new journey,
With a brand new start.

Joyous day

O joyous day,
When Jesus washes the past away,
When in his loving arms and his wings,
My heart and soul now at peace,
Assured bursts forth and sings,
It tells of his loving ways his tender hand,
Unfathomable depths I do not yet understand,
Gently guiding with his love,
A love so tender a love so pure,
As I gaze at the sky of hues azure,
I look around with childlike eyes,
Amazed at all the grandeur,
As I view the word with surprise,
I see such beauty as I find rest,
Life is a miracle and if we endure the test,
God can bring a healing in every way,
That he alone knows best.

Destiny

I was standing on the shores of destiny,
They were glistening amongst the pebbles of life,
I was listening for the voice of change and peace to replace the silent scream of living,
Suddenly I felt an inner peace and saw the brightness of salvation,
The voice was calling me to be still and to be at one with nature and to be near to my creator,
As the waves tossed and turned my pebbles of the past into slivers of sand falling through my fingers,
I saw a glimpse of heaven as the sun pushed away clouds of doubt and out danced the tears of rain,
The tears were replaced with glorious sunshine filled tomorrows,
My life is but a grain of sand shimmering, shining being refined as gold,
I am inside the potters hand being moulded by a skilful,
Masterful yet gentle master,
I know one day I will see the potter at his wheel creating masterpieces out of nothing,
Until that day I will stand on the shores of destiny,
I am realizing that it is my decision and for me to grasp the outstretched hand from heaven,
I need to understand that there's a rock called the rock of recovery found in the sea of dreams,
It is my decision to grasp and touch heavens gate of gold and to approach the throne of grace,
For now I will view the shores of destiny and wait upon my Lord,
Until like the eagle I can renew my strength and soar through the mountain tops named hope.

Look for me

Look for me and you will find me,
Search for me I am here,
I am not far away open your eyes so that you can see me,
Do not be afraid for I am right next to you,
When you are anxious do not fear,
When you are feeling lonely when you think you are all alone,
I am praying for you interceding for you on my heavenly throne,
When you are feeling exiled when you are feeling lost and out on a limb,
That's when doors are waiting to be opened that's when you will have new beginnings,
New songs placed within your heart as I remove the barrier of sin,
When you look for me you will find me when you seek me with all your heart,
Do not look left or right from the narrow way do not depart,
I am always here I have never left you,
I will be here for you waiting when your journey is complete.

I had a glimpse of heaven

I had a glimpse of heaven whilst I was sleeping,
There was not any sighing there was not any weeping,
At the gates of heaven the angels were keeping,
While I was there dreaming angels faces were beaming,
I knew that heaven was a special place both for me and you,
That when we pass on by this earthly life,
We will see heavens lovely view,
The harps will be there playing as palm trees will be swaying,
In an eternity of living as our spirits are made new,
I had a glimpse of heaven saw it with my own eyes,
Its beauty and its riches should come as no surprise,
For as God takes care of us in our earthly walk as we seek and do h is will,
We know he is forever faithful and his promises he does fulfil,
He promises a room in heaven where he has prepared a place,
I know one day I will see him and see his lovely face,
I had a glimpse of heaven I saw beyond the cloud,
Where the whispering of angels will one day be shouted out aloud,
As God calls us home as we are homeward bound.

I am with you

I am with you always,
I was with you yesterday, today and I will be with you tomorrow,
No matter what happens I will be with you,
For my love for you is constant in the dawning of a new day,
I am there at the setting of the sun,
My presence does not leave you,
In your sadness and in your happiness,
I will be by your side,
If you are living in poverty or wealth I will provide for you,
In your failure and success I will be waiting with open arms,
I am here to share in all your dreams, in your hopes,
I am here to s hare in all your aspirations,
I am here in all your sufferings I was on the cross for you,
I am now at the right hand side of the father interceding for you,
I am here for you.

Joy

Welling up within my being,
Living streams of happiness seem to extend beyond what I can ever dream,
Rivers of honey, rivers of splendor,
Envelop my heart,
As motherhood approaches and I know this is just the start,
Of the beauty of God and his blessings that are poured out which will not depart.

Healer

Great healer of our bodies, minds and souls,
Thank you for your loving and gentle touch,
Yet we are mortal and not complete until in heaven you call us home,
You reach down to us from heavens throne,
With compassion in your heart and tears of love flowing from your eyes,
Your hand of love reaches us from heavens skies,
To give us a glimpse of all that we will be,
When we will be with you eternally.

Praise

I will praise you on the mountain top,
I will declare of all you have done for me,
I will tell how you laid down your life for the sin you could see,
Now I am not a captive to sin I am completely free,
I will declare my love for you,
I will declare my love on high,
For you o Lord and savior gave up life,
So I do not have to die,
I thank you Lord with all my heart you died and rose again,
You are now in heaven where you will forever reign.

Through the eyes of a child

I wish I could see my God as though I was seeing him through the eyes of a child,
Unspoilt, uncorrupted pure and innocent with a willingness to trust,
I wish I could stretch out my hands to my heavenly father and hold his
hand when unsure and afraid,
I wish I could run into his arms to be held when I am confused and upset,
I wish I could tell him all my hopes and dreams and see him smile,
I wish I could call him abba and know in my heart that he is daddy,
I wish I could hear him encouraging when I feel that I have failed and I
wish I could see him wiping my tears away when life gets hard,
I wish I could realize God is only a prayer away,
To know that no matter where I think my relationship with him is going,
To know that I am still his child as he longs to help me on my journey,
That he wants to fill my heart with joy,
That he wants me to soar like the eagle on the mountain top,
I can be my fathers' child right now I can reach out to him,
I do not need to wish these things for today they can be a reality through prayer.

The angels

The angels were smiling as they spread their wings across an azure sky,
The earth was as it should be quiet and peaceful evil was no more,
Sin was no more, sickness and death was no more,
All lived in an earthly paradise where no one grew old,
All was harmonious all was calm as it was deemed by the creator,
The angels stretched their wings and were silent for a while,
They could hear children playing laughing innocent and pure,
The angels gazed at a land which had not seen war for a thousand years,
A land where the lion and the lamb lay side by side and men walked
amongst that which the creator had created,
They were walking without either man or the animals being perturbed,
There was not a single cloud in the sky,
Had not been for a long long time,
Since the new earth had been created with Satan defeated and chained life
on earth was good,
Mankind no longer struggled with the problems of yesterday but enjoyed all
that was good,
No one could remember what sickness, death or misery was like,
For it had all passed and this was the way mankind wanted this idyllic life to stay.

One Day at a time

I will live one day at a time Lord,
I will entrust it all to you,
For you are the creator of all things for when I found you,
You made me brand new,
You taught me not worry or to fret and to walk with you each day,
You showed me to accept you as my Lord and saviour,
The life the truth the way,
To be planted in the vine,
To know you is divine,
I will live one day at a time Lord,
I will entrust it all to you,
For days spent in your presence have a beautiful and splendid view.

In the stillness

In the stillness I can feel his presence and feel so close,
I could almost touch his hand,
I can hear his sweet soft voice as he speaks across the land,
How can I doubt my saviour is real as I look at this world again and again,
For his name holds power and he is miraculous and spoken of highly by men,
I long to meet my saviour I long to gaze at his face,
I long to run and win the race by his mercy and his grace,
I long to talk with him telling him about my day,
I long to give my all to him and in his presence stay,
If only I had a second left I would want to be with him,
I would spend eternity of eternity which today does begin,
I long not to rush leaving my saviour behind,
For he is my Lord and master and I should never forget the day we first met,
He saved my life and rescued me and gave me life beyond all measure and
he is my greatest treasure,
He broke my chains and set me free,
With a quiet still voice he speaks and leads me,
I walk down to the path of salvation it was meant to be,
For the rest of my days I want to be with the angels giving my Lord my praise,
I want to see the roof of splendour begin to raise,
When I am feeling down and burdened with life's cares and woes,
When I am in the midst of foes,
I can turn to My Lord and saviour for he is the only one,
He knows my heart and how to comfort me,
His arms are warm and tender,
He gives me strength, he gives peace like a dove and speaks to my soul
saying let it be.

Joy rising

Joy is rising from deep within my soul,
Joy is a river of honey making me whole,
Joy is sweetness itself,
Filling me with gladness restoring my health,
With joy overwhelming my being,
I am richer than the richest crown belonging to any king,
With joy inside me it is better than the loveliest song a blackbird could ever sing,
With joy from my Lord Jesus he gives the very best,
For joy is the fruit of the spirit that he promises to invest.

Heavens gift

You are heavens gift to me,
You mean the world to me,
I cannot think what I did before you were around,
Now blessings in their fullness truly abound,
Your smile just melts my heart,
I cannot comprehend or thank God enough for this new start,
It seems like my life is new,
The pain of yesterday has gone and it is all because of you,
I am amazed at what god has done for he has blessed me with you,
How did I live before I knew his son,
He has given me the treasures and desires of my heart,
It is no longer longing or missing a part,
I thank God with all of my being,
For when I look at you new beginnings are seen,
Finally I feel complete Gods given me an angel to keep,
You are so beautiful it makes me want to weep,
Not with tears of sadness but with tears of gladness and joy,
I will love you more each day and as our lives unfold,
They will reveal the richest memories that joyously can be told.

Thank you Lord for joy

Thank you for happiness,
Thank you for laughter,
Thank you for all the reasons I will submit to you my Lord and master,
Thank you for the sunshine,
Thank you for the rain,
Thank you for being in my life for taking away the pain,
Thank you for creation thank you for the trees,
Thank you for your grace and mercy when I am on my knees,
Thank you for the oceans,
Thank you that you are in control,
Thank you for being you for making me whole,
Thank you that the battle has already been won,
But thank you most of all for Jesus your precious and one and only son.

One day

One day you are returning,
One day you will be here,
To restore us to bring you glory,
To remove from crying eyes and hearts every single tear,
I cannot wait for that wonderful day,
When you will return and people will pray,
They will accept you as saviour,
It may happen at night it may happen at day,
No one will know when you are coming but Lord I Pray,
Let it be soon so evil is sent on its way.

You make my joy complete

As I hold you in my arms I get a glimpse of heaven,
As I hold you close where love surrounds me,
As I feel content,
While I look at your eyes of innocence,
I know that I am truly blessed and I praise the Lord with all my heart,
With all that's deep within my spirit and my soul I give thanks to my
heavenly father,
When I hold you close to me what makes me think is how you are is all we
are meant to be pure and loving unconditionally,
I know when I look into your eyes my heart just melts,
I feel love and joy deep within my being,
For when I hold you dear my joy is complete.

A life without love

A life without love cannot be called living,
It has no quality without love, laughter or giving,
Today's special moments with all of its pleasures,
Soon become yesterdays memories with immeasurable treasures,
Treasures that have the value of silver and gold that help the soul remain
youthful as our lives they unfold,
My life's journey I would like to share with you,
As paths walked with a partner have a wonderful view,
A beautiful world more vivid than dreams,
Is one I envisage with babbling brook streams,
Streams like our lives crystal and clear,
A life spent together we need no longer fear,
As time passes ice capped mountains can melt,
As does my heart with feelings heart felt.

The wilderness

I am walking through the darkness,
I am holding Jesus hand,
I am walking through the wilderness into the promised land,
I know it will not be easy but Jesus will carry me through,
For he went through much more suffering than I could do,
To secure his fathers children's place in heaven,
By his mercy and his grace.

Suffering

To live without suffering means we are not living,
To share in the gift of the cross were God is forgiving,
To know the love of Jesus with his arms open wide,
To have him hold our hand when we are fearful and wearisome,
To know the healing of Gods own precious son,
To walk life's path with God by our side,
Is to have our eyes opened when once we were blind,
For its then we have a glimpse of heaven and the angels above,
Its when Jesus shares our sufferings that we truly know love.

Lord you died for me

Lord you died for me at Calvary,
You gave your life to set me free,
You broke the chains of iniquity,
You sacrificed everything for me,
You died on the cross without dignity,
Your hands and feet bound and nailed,
Your victory over death and evil has prevailed,
Your true majesty and glory unveiled,
You will return to earth again,
You will bring true peace and love and end all pain.

Lukewarm?

Are you lukewarm when you follow me?
When you walk past the homeless do you see what I see?
Or do you walk on by?
Focussing on your own misery?
Do you reach out to those who need a helping hand?
Or do you bow your head and avert your gaze?
Or do you pray that I will forgive you and understand?
Do you reach out to those whom others would scorn?
Do you notice the lost and the shoe that is severely worn?
Would you give them a drink of water as you passed them in the street?
Would you show such kindness or hastily retreat,
Would you extend your arms with love to such people such as these?
Would you lay aside your prejudices or would you only help when only you
would choose to please?
Would you walk along the street with them and share the good news?
Or are you content to place church in a box and sit there in your pews?
Are you prepared for a challenge that I have prepared for you?
Or are your ears hardened with your heart?
That one day you will you will say to me Lord I never listened or sought the
plans you were asking me to do?

Father as we ask

Father as we ask for eyes that truly see your majesty,
Teach us to desire a mind that opens eagerly,
As we praise your name let our hearts respond joyously,
Give us ears that listen earnestly as we seek your will,
Draw near to us as we are still,
May our mouths witness truthfully as we live our lives for you,
Lets store eternal treasures as the spirit makes us new.

Eternity

Endless days of eternity breathed and given by God,
Starts now,
A free gift of heaven for us to enjoy,
Special moments and memories as if frozen and suspended in time,
If we choose to rest for a while,
I spent time absorbing the majestic experiences as a swan and her cygnets
pass by on a lake pool of wildlife blessed by God,
The swan the commander and guardian of life,
Its very essence of beauty and grandeur,
Enthrals and captures my attention for a while,
I day dream in the late spring evening taking in and capturing a snapshot of heaven.

Destined

Destined to hope destined to dream,
Destined to search destined to glean,
Something wonderful from God above,
Destined to experience his endless love,
Destined to find his promises are true,
To see the colours of the rainbow in every single hue,
Destined to walk life with its twists and its turns,
Destined to find out that Gods heart yearns,
Fo us to love and to trust him and to tell him our fears,
Destined once we have found him to follow him for years,
Destined to be chosen destined to be saved,
To find out its all part of gods plan and aim,
Destined to find Jesus and why our saviour came,
Destined to have revealed the victory God has won,
Through his own precious son,
Destined to hold angels hands in the heavenly realm,
Destined in the storms of life to have God at the helm.

Especially

I am especially yours when I am quiet and my heart is at rest,
After I have gone through trials, when my faith has been put to the test,
When I can see beyond the walls of doubt and beyond my fears,
You start to reveal your purpose that you have been telling me for years and years,
To reach the lonely and to reach the lost,
To give back to you all my praise by sharing with others who need you and
to do this all my days,
Although at the moment I do not know how this will be,
I cannot know the plans fully or what you foresee,
The plans are yours and I know I must trust you and not let go,
For when we do this the covenant we make,
Let us see your promises as they begin to show.

Clearing the temple grounds

Lord am I bringing the best of what I have to church or second best?
Is what I am offering unblemished or tarnished?
Is what I am bringing from a pure heart with pure motives?
To bring you glory and to worship you sacrificially?
Or for my own designs, and desires of my heart?
Is what I am presenting to you authentic and true?
Or a myriad of confusion among the temple grounds?
Does this Signify that whilst I am searching to find, what I think I should bring with me to church,
That somehow I am missing the very essence of what you are conveying to me?
That my whole life should be worship and a complete sacrifice,
Not just an outward sign of an offering.

Lord I thank you

Lord I thank you for all creation,
For every flower and every bird,
As your wind powerfully stirs me,
The wind speaks to me of all that I have heard,
That everything in all creation has a purpose, has a plan
If we rush and miss the beauty,
Then we will rush and miss the peace,
For all you offer is in your creation,
Let us not forget this daily blessing,
For when we trust and cease,
Then you reveal to us your perfect and precise blessings,
In your perfect timing,
Endless joy you do release.

The Banquet

A large group of people were gathering outside the gates of heaven- a discussion shortly followed and one man said "I shall go in first, I am the most important so I will dine in the prime position at the banquet table." "Excuse me, I have great wealth so I should go first." Said the second man indignantly.

"The King will welcome me for I have great status and power – only I can go in", the third man insisted.

"My dear men, I have great intellect and wisdom, I will go and dine with the King," the fourth man said.

These men felt very proud as they waited – the King would be impressed at what fine guests he had invited they thought.

Their gaze fell upon a man who had said nothing whilst they were talking. The man was dressed in rags.

"We have come in all our finery but you have come in rags. The King will send his servants to send you away. We have great wealth, status, power, intellect and wisdom.

They asked: What gifts have you to give to the king?"

The man replied, "Indeed you see I do not have the wealth of men yet I am truly rich. As for status and power, it is true I have little yet I am truly free because of one that is greater than me.

As for intellect I am not what you could term a scholar and the wisdom of men I have little,

But the one I seek possesses all wisdom and intellect beyond all reasoning.

"You haven't answered our question, " said the men, "What gifts have you to give to the King?"

The man replied, "I have already given him the most precious gift I have"

"What is that?" asked the men.

The man smiled, "Well I have given Jesus my heart"

Let us not forget the price that Jesus paid
By laying down his life the greatest sacrifice was made
With nails in his hands and feet as he hung on the tree
He died to set you and me free
No one can equal the love that he gave
The sinner he came to save
He has opened the doorway to Gods special love
Now lets join with angels and lift our praises above

Gods perfect love amazes me all creation declares his majesty all heaven and earth at his command guided by his loving hand
I watch the sunrise as it lights the day may gods love like the sunrise show the way happiness and joy gods love does bring like birds of the dawn my heart does sing with praise and thanks ill start the day
Gods perfect peace amazes me peace that is given to you and me may gods peace fill us as we pray let us show the world a different way
As we walk gods chosen path let him join our day while we meet both friend and foe
let us share the love we know lets pray that our heart and mind reveals gods peace to all mankind
Gods perfect gift of life amazes me he sent a savior to set us free Jesus removed the barrier of sin he sent the holy spirit to dwell within
Jesus prince of peace and king of kings let us bring our lives as offerings let us know your will
Let us accept gods gift of grace and let our hearts be still

God sent his son to cleanse us from sin
Forgave us restored us to let the holy spirit dwell within
Gods patient and forgiving his love never ends
His peace flows freely it always transcends
Transcends all understanding transforms my heart
Releases his power gives the world a new start
may gods love and peace rain down on earth
let us join angels singing of our saviors birth

Lightning Source UK Ltd.
Milton Keynes UK
31 August 2010

159232UK00001B/5/P